Elijah Davidson
and the Oregon Caves

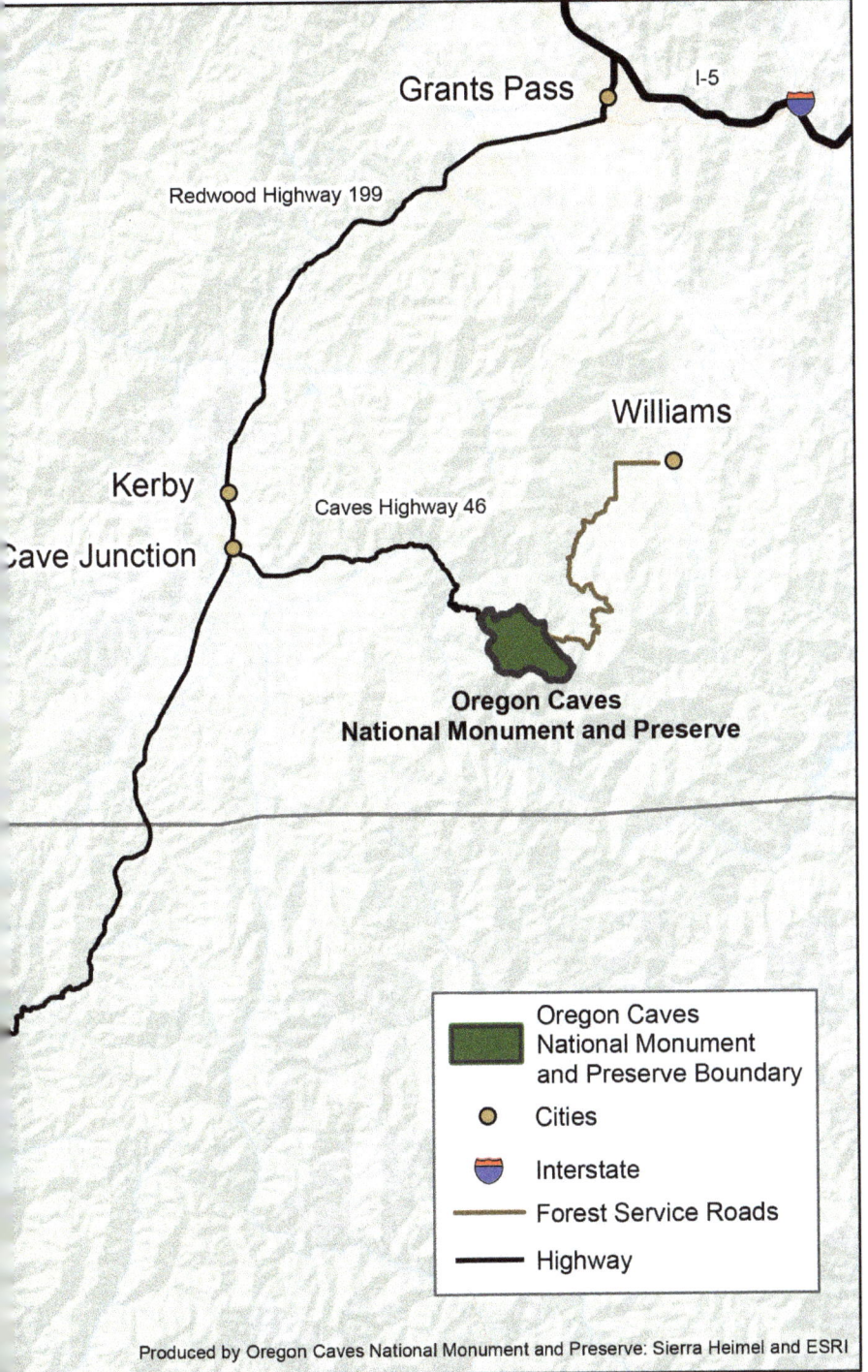

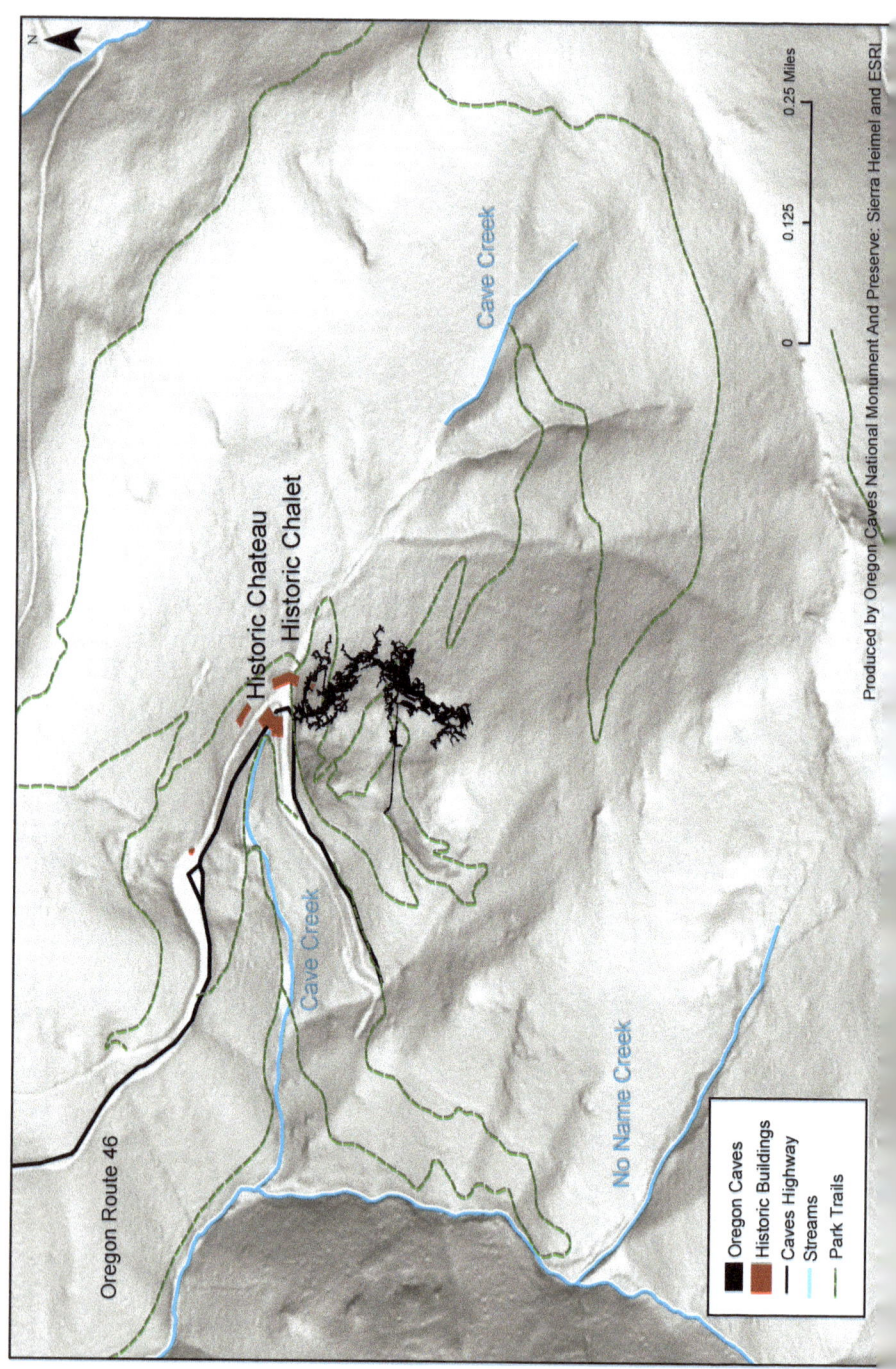

Elijah Davidson
and the Oregon Caves

Tom Siewert
with Irma Thompson

LEFT FORK
Illinois Valley • Oregon

Elijah Davidson and the Oregon Caves

Copyright © 2024 Tom Siewert

All rights reserved. No part of this book may be reproduced by any means without permission.

Cover photo courtesy of OCNM & P, Museum and Archives Collections

Maps on previous pages produced by Oregon Caves National Monument and Preserve: Sierra Heimel and ESRI.

ISBN-13 (Paperback): 978-1-945824-62-3

First Left Fork Edition: February 2024

10 9 8 7 6 5 4 3 2 1

Left Fork
PO Box 110
O'Brien, OR 97534
www.leftforkbooks.com

CONTENTS

INTRODUCTION	IX
PROLOGUE Discovery	1
CHAPTER ONE Elijah Davidson's Family History and Early Life	9
Focus: Setting The Scene	12
CHAPTER TWO The Middle Years	15
Focus: Making A Cave	22
CHAPTER THREE The Later Years and Becoming a National Monument	25
Focus: Flora And Fauna	37
CHAPTER FOUR Questions and Details	41
Focus: Native People Of The Caves' Region	50
CHAPTER FIVE Irma's Tale	53
CONCLUSION	65
APPENDIX I A Timeline of Events for Oregon Caves and Elijah Davidson	69
APPENDIX II History of the Discovery of the Marble Halls of Oregon	75

INTRODUCTION

Few people who visit Oregon Caves National Monument go away not knowing the name of Elijah Davidson. His story has become integral with the experience of cave tours there; the fears he faced, and the sense of adventure, of exploring the darkness with only a few matches, are what link many people to this remote underground realm. Who was this man who discovered the cave? This account will try to answer that question and provide some insight into this simple man whose story gets told with every cave tour given, hundreds of times each year. Included here you will find some basic information about his life and family, as well as stories that help to illustrate the essence of this man, this place, and the times in which they came together.

In 2001, when I began working as a guide at Oregon Caves National Monument, I grew fascinated with Elijah's story and began researching the man and his history. I traveled from the Caves, north to the state of Washington, down to California, and over to the area of Williams, Oregon, interviewing some of the last living people who knew Elijah. Much of the information herein is the result of my research, doing personal interviews, visiting historical societies and libraries, and experiencing the places involved in the story. I will try to flesh out the facts of this man, his story, and his family history, a history that sheds light on the time in which he lived.

The book begins with a Prologue in which I present a dramatic version of the discovery of Oregon Caves, based mostly on previous accounts, as well as creatively filling in some gaps in the story. Chapter One discusses Elijah Davidson's early life and family, as well as the circuitous route that brought him to southern Oregon. Chapter Two continues Elijah's story with his middle years, from his marriage to the discovery of the Caves. Then we look at Elijah's later years and some important events in subsequent Oregon Caves history, including its naming as a national monument. Chapter Four presents answers to some commonly asked questions at the Caves, as well as some other details that didn't fit into other places in the book. Along the way through these chapters you will find Focus sections on Caves geology, flora, fauna, and the Native peoples of the region. Chapter Five belongs to Irma Thompson, Elijah's granddaughter, who presents her recollections of Elijah and the area. Then I conclude the main body of the book. Following the conclusion you will find an appendix with both a human history timeline and Elijah's 1922 telling of the discovery of the Caves. I hope you enjoy this voyage into Oregon Caves history.

One item to note in reading this work, is that I often use the words Cave and Caves as proper names to represent Oregon

Caves. When I use the lower case 'cave' it is to signify a cave in the general sense. Also, there is only one main cave at Oregon Caves, but the reason the plural is used is due to there being multiple entrances to the Cave, which at one time were thought to be different caves.

*Entrance to Oregon Caves in winter
(Photo courtesy of OCNM & P, Museum
and Archives Collections)*

*Elijah Davidson with his old muzzle loading percussion rifle
(Photo courtesy of OCNM & P, Museum
and Archives Collections)*

PROLOGUE

Discovery

His feet pounded the ground as he made his way through tall brush up the steep incline on the flanks of Sand Mountain.* In syncopation to that rhythm, the bellows in his chest pushed in and out as fast as they could, and the drumming of his pulse in his ears added a third rapid beat. "Bruno," he called, eyes scanning the slope for the canine companion that had taken off after who knows what other animal, just after they had subdued the deer. He felt the weight of his muzzle-loading percussion rifle in his hand, the bouncing of his ammunition pack against his hip, and the cold autumn air on his cheeks and in his lungs. He heard the barking of his faithful friend, now somewhat muffled, a short ways ahead.

First he saw the stream that seemed to come out of nowhere, appearing from between the rocks and brush. As he glanced to his right, the direction from which a deep

---

* *Sand Mountain was an early name for what we now call Mount Elijah, the mountain wherein the Cave has formed.*

growl and series of barks emerged, he caught sight of a dark hole behind the scrub of Oregon grape and ocean spray. Approaching, now slowly and carefully, he listened with piqued attention as the cacophony of growling and barking seemed to fade into the mountain itself. He looked in bewilderment at the opening in the rocks and debated whether or not to enter. The dog was a good hunter and companion, one he felt loath to lose, but entering such a dark recess, knowing that an angry bear lurked somewhere inside, could mean not making it back to Minerva, Anna Geneva, and Winter, his kith and kin.

His moment of indecision came to an abrupt end when he heard a loud, high-pitched yelp spring from the cavern before him. He set down his rifle – too long and cumbersome in such a small place – pulled out his knife and grabbed some matches from his pouch. He broke off a few, struck them on the rocks, and lit the way ahead of him into a dark, damp underground realm. He paused for a moment just inside the hole to let his eyes adjust to the twilight. In the enclosed space, the smell of the sulfur matches stung his nostrils, but he hardly noticed, for what lay before him held his concentration. He looked down at the floor of the small room in which he crouched, and saw the telltale sign of a bear having slept there. Creeping onward, he heard echoes of the stream inside the walls of stone, and soon came to the water's edge. Crawling among the rocks to avoid getting his feet soaked in the cold water, he made his way, matches and knife in hand, past uneven walls of ghostly shapes. Never had he seen such a place, but the growl of the bear brought him back to the matter at hand.

His matches burned down to his fingertips and he pulled out the block and broke off some more. Holding them up to see as well as possible, he pushed onward, listening for dog or bear, his concentration broken now and then by the odd looking white and tan rocks that glistened in the dancing light. He continued in this manner until he realized he was down to the last of the matches, his only source of light. Intrigued by the possibility of seeing more, he realized that it would have to wait for another time. The immediate problem was to get out of the cave alive. He turned and began to retrace his steps, but it all looked so completely different from the other direction, that he wasn't certain through which of the maze of passageways he had come. He found his foot- and handprints in some soft earth, but just as he began to follow them, the matches died, and with them died his only light. The dark engulfed him like a tidal wave and he stopped in his progress, dumbfounded by the total absence of any viable direction.

He thought of Bruno and of the bear. He thought of his relatives expecting him back at camp soon. He thought of his family waiting for him in their Williams Valley home, his wife Minerva and children Anna Geneva and Winter Lynn. As the face of fear thrust itself into his imagination, he sat down, rocks poking into his spine from several angles. He began to wonder if anyone could find him before it was too late. Just then, a rushing sound came to his attention. The stream. He knew if he could get back to the stream he could find his way out of this rather disheartening predicament. He moved his head around, cupping his ears to try and determine the likely direction of the water. When he thought he had pinpointed it, he began to crawl, one hand on the ground and one out ahead of him feeling for the shape of the passageway.

His knees complained at their contact with rocks, but he pushed onward, ignoring the pain. His clothes caught on the narrow walls, frustrating his efforts, but still he kept moving. Stopping now and then to listen for the water and check his direction, he gladdened to the increasing sound of the stream. It seemed that voices rose from the gurgling waters: those of his fellow hunters, or just imagination? He kept moving, calling out now and then to Bruno, to his brothers. The sound of the bear had faded. On the one hand that comforted him, but on the other it brought hair on the back of his neck to attention. Where was the brute now? He had no choice but to continue as best he could.

The sound of the stream grew ever louder until, glad for the hope of emerging again into light, he felt cold running water on his fingertips. He increased his pace, but slowed when his head reminded him of the uneven shape of the rock walls and ceilings. He had to leave the stream bed in a few places due to the narrowness of the openings – he didn't want to squeeze into places and be totally underwater for an unknown period of time. Eventually he saw in the distance, a faint glow of light that indicated his success in returning to the world of the living. Still moving cautiously, he walked through the cold, swift water, and in a short time he had to shield his eyes from the bright light of day. By this time it had become more the light of evening, for the sun had neared the western horizon. When his eyes adjusted he looked to the West and estimated his time underground at a shade under three hours. It was the longest three hours he would ever remember.

He sat down and thanked the Good Lord that he had returned to safety. What about Bruno; was he still in the cave? He grabbed his rifle and strode down the hill to where the dead deer lay. He knelt, hoisted the buck onto his right shoulder and trudged up the slope until he stood at the cave entrance once again. He lay the carcass down, and as he turned and began to head down the hill, he heard a familiar bark behind him. Bruno ran down the slope, limping a bit on his left foreleg, but smiling his pleasure at seeing his human friend once again. The dog had some nasty cuts, but they would heal in good time. For now, the two were just so glad to see one another that the hunter didn't mind the face washing he got from his four-legged friend. The sun had just about dipped below the horizon as they set out for camp.

When they glimpsed the campfire in the distance they could see there wasn't too much activity; the other intrepid hunters, trusting their friend's knowledge of the woods and his capabilities, had all hit the sack except one, his brother Carter. "You look a bit the worse for wear. It's about time you found your way back, and empty handed at that." In between mouthfuls of stew Carter had kept warm for him, the hunter recounted his adventure of the afternoon. Carter had never known his brother to be a teller of tall tales, but this sure seemed like one. Still, Elijah did look like he'd had quite a time of it, and Bruno was scratched pretty badly in a few places. After the tale, Carter just shook his head and bid his brother goodnight. Elijah let the food settle for a while after his brother had gone to his bedroll, then washed Bruno's cuts before he, exhausted, crawled into his own bedroll for a sound night's sleep.

The next day after breakfast Elijah headed back to the Cave entrance with Bruno. Most of the party had just grinned in disbelief when he told them about the previous afternoon's adventure, but his brother-in-law Jules Goodwin was intrigued enough to join him in returning to the cave. When they neared the place where he had shot the deer, they could already hear the singing of the stream as it poured from the cave. In a short time they caught sight of the entrance and Elijah pointed in its direction. "You see that black spot? That's my bear." It had eaten a good chunk of the deer carcass and lay engorged on the ground in front of the black hole. Just as Elijah had described, Jules saw two dark holes in the side of the mountain, one with the stream emerging from it.

They tried to awaken the bear, but he was so groggy that their taunts produced only a few lazy movements and some half-hearted groans. Finally Elijah shot the bruin and began dressing him out, but not before he took Jules a short ways into the cavern to confirm his story. By the light of Jules' matches they stood in awe of the amazing passageways and rock features that Elijah had had little chance to appreciate the day before. So the story was, indeed, true, and not a tall tale as the others, and Jules to be honest, had assumed. Elijah had found a cave.

That hunter's name was Elijah Jones Davidson, and on that day in the autumn of 1874, he became the first human known to have entered the hallowed walls of Oregon Caves. Until Elijah Davidson lit a bundle of Chinese sulfur matches and illuminated the total darkness of those marble halls, the rocks and creatures of this gem in the Siskiyou Mountains of southwestern Oregon had possibly never known that light even existed.

*Elijah Davidson in his youth
(Photo courtesy of OCNM & P, Museum
and Archives Collections)*

CHAPTER ONE

Elijah Davidson's Family History and Early Life

Elijah Jones Davidson entered this world in Schuyler county, Illinois, on January 22, 1849. His family tree traces back to Scotland just a few generations earlier. Grandfather Elijah Davidson, born in 1783, hailed from Rutherford County, North Carolina, and father Elijah Barton Davidson was born in Glasgow, Barron County, Kentucky, in 1819. The latter married Saloma Jones, so "our Elijah" bore the first and last name of his father and grandfather, and his middle name came from his mother's family. Saloma also had a brother named Elijah, so he represented both sides of the family equally.

Elijah's family was involved in the Restoration Movement, a religious reform movement that began in the early 1800s and sought to "bring the church back into alignment with biblical principals." The Davidsons apparently belonged to the Campbellite group, who often prefer to be called simply "Christian," that later gave birth to a sect today called the Church of Christ or Christian Church. Grandfather Elijah decided to move the family west, so in 1850 they left Illinois and traveled the Oregon Trail with wagons pulled by oxen, part of a larger group of like-minded intrepid Christians from their church. Elijah Jones Davidson had thirteen siblings, one of whom, a boy named Ivory, died on the trail, and four others who never lived to adulthood. In those days, large families meant more hands to contribute to the hard labor of farming, not to mention the fact that it gave more certainty to having a decent number of them survive.

Elijah Barton Davidson (Photo courtesy of Bruce Thompson)

The family settled first in Portland, Oregon. Grandpa Elijah had a 160-acre land grant around what is now Laurelhurst Park. That would be a pretty valuable piece of property today, but the family did not stay. Elijah's niece claims they moved away because they "never thought Portland would amount to much," but most likely there were other, more legitimate reasons for them having moved. Her statement does add a nice touch of irony and humor to the story, however.

In defense of her statement, though, Portland at the time was a new, small, and rather rough place to live. In its first census, that of 1850, Portland boasted 821 people: 653 males, 164 females, and 4 "free colored" individuals. Though still very much a frontier town, it was the largest one in the Northwest at the time, often nicknamed

"Stumptown" or "Mudtown," due to logging and weather conditions respectively. Nonetheless, Portland grew quickly, once it got started, and became incorporated as a city in 1851. By 1900 there were 90,000 residents and it was the largest city in the Pacific Northwest.

Whatever their reason for leaving, in 1855 the Davidsons moved farther south and, along with others of the church, founded the town of Monmouth, Oregon, named for the town from which they had left in Illinois. Grandpa Elijah later became one of the founders of Monmouth University, which today bears the name of Western Oregon University. The Davidson family became an integral part of the growing town of Monmouth, but Elijah Jones' parents, Elijah Barton and Saloma Jones Davidson, decided to take their family farther south in 1866. They apparently sought to obtain one of the land grants in California, but didn't quite make it to that state. Instead they settled in the Applegate Valley at a place known as Missouri Flat, across the river from Williams, Oregon, and closer to what now bears the name Provolt. At the time only about a dozen families made up the Williams community. Land and resources were plentiful, not to mention beautiful, so there they stayed.

Focus: Setting The Scene

The story of how the mountain and the Cave came to exist goes back well before Elijah and Bruno ever ventured there. Just over 200 million years ago, the area that now comprises Oregon Caves and the Siskiyou Mountains sat close to a type of geologic fault where one part of the Earth's crust was thrust over another. The sea covered most of this land, and volcanoes stood nearby occasionally spewing lavas. Just below sea level, mats of algae produced a mineral known as calcite, calcium carbonate, that formed limestone on the underlying rocks, eventually building up to hundreds of feet thick over time.

This limestone was then forced underneath the continent where they were changed into marble. Marble and limestone are chemically about the same, but limestone is a sedimentary rock, whereas marble is metamorphic. Much later the marble was uplifted forming mountains, that geologists call the Klamath Mountains, but most local people call the Siskiyous. Evidence indicates that they are still slowly rising. The heat and pressure that changed the limestone into marble and the interesting geologic history these rocks have undergone has given us the veins of gold, silver, copper, and other minerals that brought many people here in the 1800s and early 1900s. Some still today seek their fortunes among those minerals, most finding more work than money.

*Ancient metamorphosed volcanic rocks along the Illinois River
(Photo courtesy of OCNM & P, Museum and Archives Collections)*

*Elijah and Minerva's wedding photo taken by Peter Britt
(Photo courtesy of the Thompson family)*

CHAPTER TWO

The Middle Years

Young Elijah Jones Davidson married Minerva Farris on July 4, 1870. A man named Peter Britt took their wedding picture. Britt became a fairly well-known photographer, taking the first photos of Crater Lake in 1874, as well as many historic photos of southern Oregon. Born in Switzerland, Britt himself came across the Oregon Trail in 1852, but after spending time in Portland he decided, like the Davidsons, to move farther south where he lived the rest of his days. A big summer-long series of concerts in Jacksonville, Oregon, bears the name "Britt Festival" in honor of the famous photographer.

The young Davidson couple farmed, but Elijah also worked as a bounty hunter and did some placer mining (panning for gold), reportedly having a claim near Gold Hill, Oregon. In November of 1871 they had their first child, Anna Geneva. After that they commenced with naming their children after the seasons. First they had a boy named Winter Lynn in October of 1873, then there were

Summer Earnest (b. Sept. 1875), Thomas Barton (b. Sept. 1877) (breaking the seasonal pattern), Autumn Forest, who preferred the name "Frank" (b. Nov. 1879), and another daughter, Vesta Pearl (b. Oct. 1883). This last girl they were going to name "Spring," but since she was born in the autumn, they didn't want anybody to "tap them for being simple," so they relented to another name.

All of the Davidson children except Frank (Autumn Forest) lived long lives. Frank reportedly had a weak constitution and passed away at the young age of 22 years, 10 months, and 22 days. His exact age is listed on his gravestone, where he is referred to as a "Woodman of the world," which was a fraternal organization started in 1890 to help people in some Western states. His is also the only gravestone in the Davidson plot to bear a poem. From all appearances he was well-loved. Life was often difficult in those days, as evidenced by the fact that in the late 1800s the average lifespan of urban Americans was less than 40 years.

Elijah built two cabins in the mountains, one on Williams Creek divide near where the modern forest road from the Caves to Williams crosses, and one on the east fork of Sucker Creek divide. He stored his traps there and would go out in the fall to set them. The name of Sucker Creek hearkens back to Elijah's origins in Illinois, for that state was nicknamed the "Sucker State" in the 1800s. One of the leading candidates for the origin of that unfortunate nickname stems from the fact that sucker fish migrate up the Mississippi River in the spring and downriver in the fall. Migrant workers paralleled that fish migration, some of them choosing to settle in the area now known as Illinois. People called those migrant workers "suckers" after the fish, hence the name applied to that state where many "suckers" settled.

Elijah spent quite a lot of his time in the mountains, due either to a great love of the natural world, a love of solitude, the fact that he felt uncomfortable in social situations, or some combination of the above. He did not offer his words freely and tended to stutter in groups of people, but was nonetheless well respected among the populace. With his friends he spoke softly and slowly. When he did open his mouth to speak, people listened. He stood only about five feet four inches tall, but was reportedly strong as an ox and had little fear of bears or anything else he encountered, except, of course, groups of people.

Elijah and Minerva had an apple orchard and grew various other crops. They planted and harvested by the moon, by natural signs, and by intuition. Once the crops were in, it seems Minerva and the children took care of them until harvest, as Elijah tended to spend his time in the hills. Elijah earned money mostly by hunting and trapping. His primary targets were bears, but he also took coyotes, bobcats, and occasionally mountain lions. Elijah became so respected as a hunter that the state issued him a perpetual hunting license. On one occasion Elijah was riding his horse through the forest and saw the characteristic claws and smooth, leather sole of a black bear paw jutting out from a hole beneath a log. He tied a rope to the pommel of his saddle, put a loop around the bear's paw, then patted his horse to pull out the bruin. The bear turned on Elijah and landed right on top of him. Elijah had his knife out and ready, and after a scuffle he subdued the bear. Not an easy way to make a living.

Not only did Elijah know how to hunt and trap, he also knew how to prepare and cook up the meat he brought home, his specialties being venison, deer and bear jerky, and bear bacon. He had his own smokehouse for such delicacies. Longtime Williams resident Louis "Babe" Fields said that his mother used to buy bear grease for cooking from Elijah. He also recalled one particular night when many of the local men were working in a mine near Elijah's house. As midnight approached, they began to wonder where "Ole Lije" had gone. Shortly thereafter Elijah reappeared announcing that dinner was ready. He fed the entire crew, and Babe commented that it was one of the best meals he had ever eaten. Irma Thompson, Elijah's granddaughter, remembered his bear jerky as tasting so delicious that she had her own little knife and would often go into the smokehouse to cut off a few mouthfuls.

The Davidson family spent time living near Bandon on the Oregon coast as well. There don't seem to be many records of their time on the coast, although the Bandon museum has a picture of Elijah along with a friend by the name of Bill Bowman. A well-known

Elijah Davidson and Bill Bowman, before they went to Alaska (Photo courtesy of Bruce Thompson)

figure in Bandon history is a man named Noah Davison, and they had Elijah's name spelled the same (Davison) even though the two, as far as is known, were not related. Elijah sometimes hunted and trapped in the Coast Ranges near Bandon while Minerva maintained the property in Williams.

One longtime Williams resident reported that her mother babysat the Davidson children. Every February there was a big fair in Roseburg and Minerva would go and sell her canned goods at the fair. The babysitter went along. In the evening, Minerva would wait outside until she heard a whistle. Then she would go and rendezvous with Elijah. When that happened, the babysitter knew there would be another little one to care for come autumn. While this story is only one person's recollection of events long before she told it to me, the birthdates of the Davidson children show they were all born in the autumn.

In 1906, after most of the children had left home, Elijah and Minerva headed to Nome, Alaska, along with Bill Bowman to try and make their fortunes in the wake of the gold rush. Bowman was a blacksmith, plumber, and jack of all trades. Accompanying them was the Davidson's youngest, Vesta Pearl, and possibly other members of the Davidson clan. Elijah did some mining and trapping, but Vesta Pearl became the center of attention. She worked in a bakery for a while. Crusty old miners who hadn't seen a pretty woman in some time reportedly would pay her gold pieces just to sit and watch her at work. The summer season brought long hours of daylight and picnics on icebergs at midnight, but winter was hard on people, with its long hours of darkness and bitter cold. Minerva fell into ill health. The family returned to Williams probably in 1909, and in 1913, Minerva succumbed to the effects of harsh Alaska climate and frontier life.

Off to Alaska: Front row from left: Bill Bowman, Elijah, Minerva, 2 unknown people, Vesta Pearl, Unknown (Photo courtesy of George and Barbara Jean Koch)

*Elijah with his wife Minerva and daughter Vesta Pearl
(Photo courtesy of Barbara Jean and George Koch)*

Focus: Making A Cave

As these mountains arose, eventually the rocks on top of the marble mostly eroded away. Water began to trickle down through cracks in the marble, and that water carried with it carbon dioxide from decaying plants in the soil. The mixture of carbon dioxide and water makes an acid, known as carbonic acid, the same one that makes the fizz in carbonated beverages. Calcite, the mineral that comprises the marble, is one of the only minerals easily dissolved in acid. Even though carbonic acid is a weak acid, given enough of it and a long time, it can dissolve out the rocks and form a cave. That is exactly what made the Oregon Caves, a process similar in some ways to how cavities form in teeth, acids dissolving the right type of mineral.

Sometime after 6 million years ago, the Cave began to form. At some point, probably around 500,000 years ago, a shift in the chemistry occurred caused by the erosion creating a large opening to the outside. That shift in the chemistry began the process of depositing calcite in the Cave instead of mostly eroding it away, producing the well-known features of such caves: stalagmites, stalactites, flowstone, popcorn, draperies and many others. The processes which have carved the Cave and deposited these formations continues in some form even today. It's a painstakingly slow, yet nonetheless dynamic and ever-changing world.

Opposite: Flowstone and drapery cave formations in Oregon Caves;
Inset: Anthodite formation in Oregon Caves
(Photos courtesy of OCNM & P, Museum and Archives Collections)

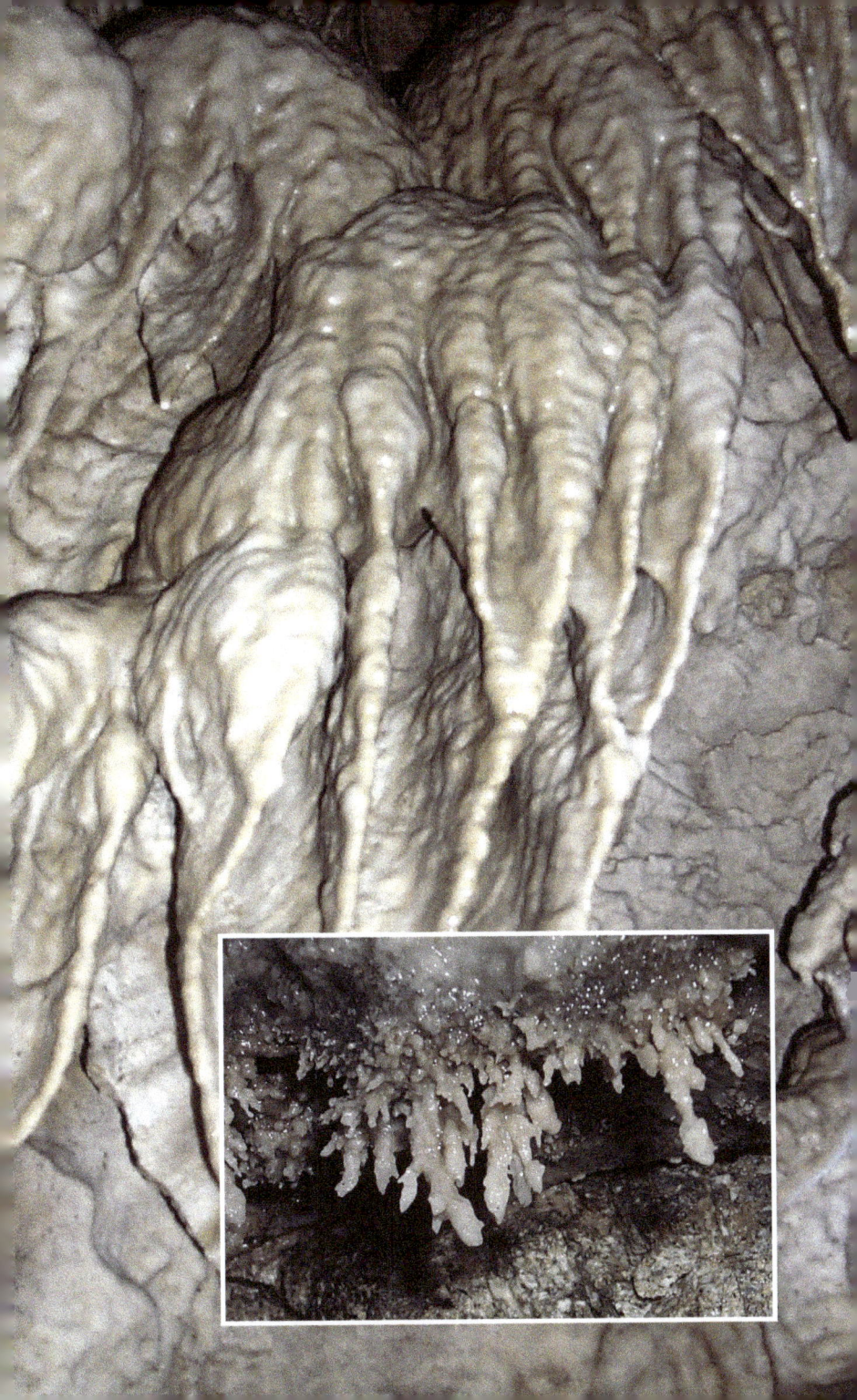

"Government Camp" tents set up near the Caves entrance, circa 1920 (Photo courtesy of OCNM & P, Museum and Archives Collections)

CHAPTER THREE

The Later Years and Becoming a National Monument

After Elijah's initial visit to Oregon Caves in 1874, he returned many other times. In 1877 he made at least two trips, one of which included William Fidler who wrote the first published account of a trip through the Cave. Not much information seems to exist regarding those later trips, other than the one with Fidler. Babe Fields recalled having traveled on horseback to the Caves with Elijah in 1920, but reporting the incident when he was eighty-nine years old he did not have many details to offer from his aged perspective. He did mention that Elijah didn't seem too pleased that the Cave had become the focus of commercial ventures, but then as mentioned earlier, Elijah never did like crowds much.

Elijah was not the only person who came to the Caves in those ensuing years. After William Fidler published his account in 1877, others became interested in the place, not the least of whom was Walter C. Burch. He, along with his partner Homer Harkness, heard about the Caves in 1884, then the two men applied for a 65 acre mining claim around the entrance to the Caves, starting in 1885. However, the only thing they were really mining was the pockets of tourists, because they began leading trips to the Caves for profit starting in that year. They put some work into the place, "improving" the route, basically enlarging the openings so people could go through without getting quite so filthy.

There are 3 main natural entrances to Oregon Caves, two of which were already mentioned, the main entrance and the carbide entrance. At some point the 110 entrance was discovered and named that because it sits about 110 feet in elevation above the main entrance. The Cave as known then, ended just past the 110. Then in 1886, Walter Burch was in the spot where the Cave ended near what is now called Niagara Falls, when he felt air movement through the passage, so he figured there was more cave beyond that point. He began trying to open the passage using small amounts of explosive. After two days of this heavy work, he crawled through the hole he had made, having to strip down to his long underwear because it was such a small passage, and was the first to find the room later called "Miller's Chapel," which will be discussed shortly, and the largest room in the Cave, the Ghost Room. Eventually he would find most of the rest of the Cave as we know it today. He increased the size of the passageways so his tourists could get through and began leading tours into the Ghost Room.

The Later Years and Becoming a National Monument

*The Harkness brothers and cave tour guests
(including William Gladstone Steel) at the entrance in 1888
(Photo courtesy of OCNM & P, Museum
and Archives Collections)*

In total, Burch spent around $1500 in exploration and improvements, a fair amount in those days, but his mining claims were always denied, because he had never completed a proper survey on the land, so he only had squatter's rights. At this time there was no road to the Caves, so the only way to get there was by horseback from Grants Pass or Williams. Burch had tents set up so visitors could spend the night, and in total the trip took people about 3 days. Visitation just wasn't high enough to make it a viable commercial venture. After a few years of leading tours and exploring the Cave, Burch gave up the business and after 1888 had little to do with the place, though he did try to claim ownership when the Caves were named a national monument.

In 1884, the same year Burch heard about the Caves, Professor Thomas Condon visited with some of his students from the University of Oregon in Eugene. Condon was originally from Ireland, but came to America with his family at a young age. He attended the Auburn Theological Seminary, was ordained as a minister, and began preaching in the early 1850s. He also had a great interest in natural history, in particular geology and paleontology. While he was tending a congregation in the Dalles, Oregon, he took some of his parishioners to survey a fossil site where they did the first survey of the location. It later became part of John Day Fossil Beds National Monument, due in large part to his work there. Though he was self-taught, Condon became the first Oregon state geologist in 1872, and in 1876 began teaching as the first professor of geology at the new University of Oregon. His students came to Jacksonville, the largest town in the area, then stopped in Williams to pick up Elijah's brother Carter to be their guide, before making their way to the Caves. They used candles for illumination, and marveled at how white and shiny the formations were, like sparkling diamonds.

In about 1890, two men from nearby Kerby, Oregon, W.J. Henderson and Frank Nickerson, along with "Captain" Alfonso Smith of San Diego located a mineral claim around the Caves site, though, like Burch, they were more interested in tourism than mining. They started the "Oregon Caves Improvement Company," to promote and lead tours of the place. By 1891 they had caught the interest of the San Francisco Examiner newspaper, who twice sent a reporter to document a tour through the Caves, in 1891 and 1894, which brought much publicity, and they were the first to use the name "Oregon Caves." Unfortunately the 1894 expedition caused considerable damage to the stalactites, stalagmites, and other formations. Smith had accrued considerable debt and disappeared in 1894, bringing an end to their money-making scheme, but they had managed to establish the route from the Illinois Valley as the easiest way to get to the Caves.

Date and initials carved in the rocks from early cave visitors. Such things were common back then, but today are not allowed. (Photo courtesy of OCNM & P. Museum and Archives Collections)

The next notable cave tour happened in 1907, when Chandler Bruer Watson and Joaquin Miller, the famed "Poet of the Sierras," visited. Upon arriving in one room, Watson decided it should be named for Miller, and has subsequently been called "Miller's Chapel." It earned the name "Chapel" in 1936, when the Grants Pass Cave Man Society held a cave man wedding in the room, complete with people wearing animal skins. In turn, Miller named the first room in the Cave Watson's Grotto.

Chandler B. Watson has some intriguing connections to Elijah Davidson, though it's not certain the two actually met. Like Elijah, Watson was born in Illinois in 1849, just a few counties separated from one another. Watson moved to Ashland, Oregon, not far from the Caves, in 1871. He graduated from the Ashland Academy in 1875 and became a U.S. deputy surveyor. Watson, like Davidson, loved the natural beauty of southern Oregon, and so he did much to protect the resources. He wrote two works on the geology of the region, *The Prehistoric Siskiyou Island* and *The Marble Halls of Oregon*, about Oregon Caves. It was Watson, probably more than anyone else, who promoted protection of the Caves, and this led to the place being named a national monument by President William Howard Taft on July 12, 1909, set aside largely for its perceived scientific value and special natural features.

The Later Years and Becoming a National Monument

Joaquin Miller
(Photo courtesy of Oregon Historical Society)

Joaquin Miller had been born Cincinnatus Hiner Miller in the midwest, but came out West where he made his fame by writing poems, stories, and newspaper articles. It's tough to find many facts about him, because he tended to treat fact rather loosely. He wrote a couple of autobiographical works, but few, if any, people consider them as factual. It is known that he attended Columbia College in Eugene, Oregon, and was admitted to the Oregon Bar in 1860, later becoming a judge in Canyon City, Oregon. For a time he owned a pony express and was the chief editor of a newspaper. Miller took his pseudonym, Joaquin, from the famous California bandit Joaquin Murietta, and even wrote an article in support of the man as a sort of Robin Hood figure. He visited England, where his poetry, Western dress, and flamboyant personality made him very popular as a representative of the American Wild West, then returned to the U.S. and continued his writing and exploring. He penned an article about his trip to the Caves, which drew national attention to the place. This article likely lent some public support to Watson's efforts in protecting the Caves. He eventually settled down in California, where he spent the rest of his days.

Naming the Oregon Caves a national monument led to the necessity of some sort of infrastructure, the first item of which was a road up the mountain. This was completed in 1922 as a dirt road, then improved over time to the winding, paved road we have today, rising nearly 3000 feet from the valley floor. The Chalet was constructed in 1923 as a lodging area and to register people for cave tours, along with some small cabins built in 1926. Interest in Oregon Caves grew, and the need for a larger lodge ensued, so they began work on the Oregon Caves Chateau, completed in 1934, which stands today as one of the great, rustic lodges of the national parks. But, we've gotten ahead of ourselves. Back to Elijah and the Cave herself.

*Oregon Caves Chateau and Chalet
with the cabins in the distance up the hill
(Photo courtesy of OCNM & P, Museum
and Archives Collections)*

In 1913 Dick Rowley, Elijah's friend from Williams, hired on as a guide at the Caves. He later became the head guide and remained in that position until 1954, when he retired at the ripe old age of eighty-five. Rowley apparently had a colorful imagination, and accounts indicate he stretched Elijah's story of the discovery, claiming that a particular dark hole in the Cave was where the discoverer had killed the bear. The two friends had a bit of a falling out over that, but Irma Thompson, Elijah's granddaughter, said she knew nothing of it and that "nobody could stay angry at Dick for very long" as he was such a good-natured man.

Left: Dick Rowley (left) and Kincaid, early cave guides; Right: A very late photo of Elijah. (Photos courtesy of OCNM & P, Museum and Archives Collections)

After Minerva's death, Elijah became more reclusive and took to spending as much time as possible in the hills, coming down for family matters and to tend the farm when he needed to do so. Elijah's son Winter came to live with his father after his mother's passing, spending the rest of his days in Williams. Summer also brought his family to live with Elijah for a time to help out on the farm. In 1926 Elijah contracted cancer, very likely cancer of the prostate, as many men succumbed to it in those days. He remained strong until the last few months before his death, and passed away quietly in 1927.

The Sparlin Cemetery, where he was laid to rest in the Davidson plot, is a beautiful, peaceful place with oak and madrone trees. In the spring, wildflowers cover the ground, especially the magenta blossoms of Indian Warrior. Summer brings hot, dry days with the farms around growing lush, looking to harvest time. In the autumn as crops reach the end of their year, oak leaves turn the color of bright sunshine and vines of poison oak add their contrast of beautiful wine red. Winter settles in with quiet, overcast days and long, cold, gentle rains. Elijah's gravestone stands near the back of the cemetery, leaning a bit due to the activity of ground squirrels, facing out over the expanse of the splendid Williams Valley that he called "home." While his body remains there, his spirit still wanders through the steep, verdant hills that he loved so dearly, where his soul found peace. What more of heaven could a person want! Go there, stay quiet, and listen. Maybe the voice that called to him will caress your heart with its gentle breath as well.

Below: Elijah Davidson's dedication at the Cave Entrance (Photo by AlbrightD, courtesy Wikimedia Commons Creative Commons 2.0; https://flickr.com/photos/100953877@N07/9939054043)

*The Davidson plot in the Sparlin Cemetery.
(Photo by Tom Siewert)*

Focus: Flora And Fauna

The entrance to the Caves sits at about 4000 feet above sea level, so it is much cooler than the valley below. Snow, sometimes quite heavy, is common throughout the winter. Today Oregon Caves is home to about 8 species of bats, some of whom make use of the cave for hibernation, as well as a multitude of smaller creatures such as springtails, cave crickets, grylloblatids (also known as icebugs), millipedes, and many others, some of whom are found no place else in the world. Odd algae, slime molds, and fungi make their homes in the Cave and many creatures from the surrounding forests wander into the dark recesses in search of food, water, or shelter. Some of those never find their way out.

Above ground on the striking slopes of the mountains, the landscape is mostly dominated by a dense old growth forest with trees such as Douglas firs, Pacific madrones, white firs, grand firs, California white oaks, incense cedars and the increasingly rare Port Orford cedars. Oregon Caves National Monument contains the most robust standing Douglas fir tree in the state of Oregon, at 13 feet in diameter. Beneath the tall trees you can find shrubs such as ocean spray, Manzanita, rhododendrons, Oregon grape, and others, and the forest floor has enough vanilla leaf and wonderful wildflowers to keep a botanist busy all summer long. In total the national monument contains nearly 400 species of vascular plants, as well as an abundance of fungi and lichens.

*Overview of the mountains around
the Caves and the Illinois Valley
(Photo by Tom Siewert)*

Of course, based on Elijah's story we would have to include both mule deer and black bears on the list of animals. Other common species include gray foxes, Siskiyou chipmunks, California ground squirrels, Douglas squirrels, mountain lions, various salamanders, including the Pacific giant salamander, and a host of birds, led by ravens, Stellar's jays, and the chipper little Oregon juncos. It is a very diverse environment, with about 150 species of vertebrates and over 200 species of arthropods. So this paltry list has barely scratched the surface of its variety, but a much larger book would be needed to do it justice.

*Tall trees near the entrance, mostly Douglas firs
(Photo courtesy of OCNM & P, Museum
and Archives Collections)*

Winter Davidson with Elijah's gun and the antlers from the deer he shot on the day of the Caves' discovery (Photo courtesy of the Thompson family).

CHAPTER FOUR

Questions and Details

The opening account of the discovery of Oregon Caves is based on Elijah's own writing of the incident. He did not actually put his story to paper until nearly fifty years after it took place, published in the *Oregon Historical Quarterly* in 1922. Memory can take many twists and turns in that amount of time, and it's likely, although not at all definite, that his account has a few facts missing and a few that changed over the years. Added to Elijah's story are elements of a 1968 recording of Elijah's niece, Stella Wetterau, telling the story as she claims to have heard it from her uncle in her youth. Of course, any good storyteller might also fill in some details that one could only imagine.

Cave guides telling the story countless times have come across a number of common questions regarding Elijah's discovery of the Cave. One of the most commonly asked questions about the discovery is, what kind of dog was Bruno? Four of the last living people who knew Elijah could not say. Elijah's granddaughter Irma Thompson said that he was very fond of Airedale terriers as hunting dogs, so it's possible that Bruno was one as well. Most of what we think of as dog breeds, however, were established by kennel clubs in the 1800s or later, so while dog breeds can be quite distinctive, it is likely that in the American West of the mid to late 1800s most dogs would not necessarily have fit the categories of what we would identify today as official breeds. So, Bruno was a bear-hunting dog, possibly related to modern Airedales, and that's all we can know for certain.

How many matches did Elijah carry with him into the Cave? Five? Six? More, or less? The number of matches would have made a big difference in how far he could have gone into the Cave. However, matches were rather different in those days than the ones we have now. Those Elijah would have carried were called Chinese sulfur matches, probably because they contained real sulfur as well as white phosphorus – the latter of which was mostly obtained from China in the 1800s, hence the name. They came in a block, sort of like a Lego piece with really long nubs, and, to use them one usually broke off several at a time. White phosphorus is highly flammable in the presence of oxygen. The matches were covered with a varnish and when one scraped them against a hard surface, the varnish seal was broken causing the phosphorus to come into contact with the air and ignite. Unfortunately, sometimes the varnish rubbed off or cracked due to drying while in one's pocket, thereby causing a difficult and potentially painful situation for the bearer. Such instability informs us as to why these matches are no longer used.

We don't know how big the block of matches was that Elijah carried, but he would likely have used several at one time as was often the case. While the number of matches could have offered us some clues as to Elijah's trip into the Cave that day, we unfortunately have no solid account of that.

What about the date? The year 1874 is the most widely quoted, and the stone at the cave entrance that bears Elijah's name cites November 23, 1874, as the date of discovery. Apparently that date originally came from Elijah's son Winter. In Elijah's own account of the discovery, again written many years after the fact, he said he wasn't certain of the date, but thought that it was October of 1873. His niece, who recounted the story of the discovery she had heard from her uncle, also used the 1874 date. Others have indicated it may have occurred in August, and still others have speculated it took place as late as 1875. Nobody knows for certain, but it was likely in 1873 or 1874, and sometime from August to November. I have settled on the November, 1874, date for this writing. The weather at that time of year at the Caves is typically cold and wet. Highs would be in the 30s – 40s °F and lows in the 20s to 30s. Snow may already have fallen, but based on more recent records, any really measurable snow would have waited until December or January. Elijah does not mention snow in his account, and in such steep terrain a snowfall would be notable, especially to a good tracker.

What was Elijah doing way up in the mountains? Visitors to Oregon Caves commonly express that question after driving up the winding road to get there. He loved the mountains, spent much time in them, and eventually had two hunting cabins not far from the Caves. On that particular trip Elijah had come into the mountains on a hunting trip with several brothers and brothers-in-law, a party of six or seven in total, including Carter Davidson and Jules Goodwin. They had gone in separate directions when they went out hunting for the day. Where they camped nobody still living knows. A likely spot could have been near Bigelow Lakes. Since the lakes lie close to the Caves, they could have found good campsites there, and they would have had abundant fresh water.

*One of the Bigelow Lakes where
Elijah's hunting party may have camped
(Photo courtesy of OCNM & P, Museum and Archives Collections)*

It is, however, not the only spot meeting those criteria. Years later a place called Pepper Camp became well known in the area. It's fairly flat, in autumn it might have a good water supply, and it's along what later became the most common route to get to the Caves from Williams, Oregon, then one of the largest communities in the area.

Some people have speculated that the bear in the story did not exist at all, partly based on the fact that it does not appear in the very brief statement on the discovery in a document by William Fidler about exploring Oregon Caves in 1877. Fiddler mentions the deer, but wrote nothing of the bear. From all accounts, however, Elijah Davidson was a fairly shy and reclusive man who stuttered in public speaking situations. He may indeed have told Fidler a rather abbreviated version of the story leaving out many details, some important.

If the bear did indeed exist, was it a black bear or a grizzly? Some early sources have debated that fact. Cave explorer Walter Burch, who ran tours into the Cave in the mid 1880s, claimed it may have been a "mealy nosed bear," which he said is a cross between a black bear and a grizzly. First, we don't know that "mealy nosed bears" actually existed. There are only anecdotal references to them (besides Burch's) dating from Elijah's time. Elijah said it was a black bear, and he hunted bears for bounty money, so he ought to have known. In Oregon, many of the black bears are brown, and since the grizzly is also called the "brown bear," the confusion has a possible point of origin.

Some have also said that the story as Elijah wrote it is too apocryphal, too similar to so many other cave discovery stories to likely have the ring of truth. Certainly having animal helpers lead us to the underworld paints a strong metaphor found in many folktales, our true animal nature leading us to the subconscious realm of mystery. It's entirely possible that the story changed over the years to reflect these somewhat universal elements. And yet, how are we supposed to find caves? Is it possible that, even though it's a fine metaphor, there exists a huge grain of fact within it? What better way to find a cave than by means of the animals who may use them as shelter?

We certainly know that Oregon Caves has been frequented by bears. No less than 5 black bear skeletons have been found therein and at least one grizzly, that one dating to over 50,000 years ago. Bears certainly do not need caves for hibernation. They will pick almost anyplace with a small amount of shelter for that purpose. A bear researcher in Shenandoah National Park in Virginia found a black bear hibernating in the hollowed top of a 50 ft. (16 m) tall oak tree. This cave in Oregon with an abundant bear population, however, would have provided a highly desirable spot for one of them to find shelter or a hibernation spot, as they would likely be doing in the cold wet autumn at 4000 ft (1250m) above sea level.

Several other accounts, including those by friends and relatives of Elijah, have stated that he did not go into the Cave after the bear. One, for instance, said that he killed the bear outside before going into the Cave. That's entirely possible. Elijah even apparently told his grandson Frank Wright when asked about going into the Cave after a wounded bear,

"Son, I expect you've heard that I might be kind of foolish, but nobody is that crazy." He apparently said something similar to a young Victor Sparlin, a resident of Williams, Oregon, who this author interviewed at the Oregon Caves. If that's true, then why did he write the story for the public stating that he did enter the Cave when the bear was still inside? In his written account he stated he did not enter the Cave chasing the bear, but just to get his dog. Maybe that's what he meant by stating that he did not chase the bear into the Cave. We can speculate all we want, but the only person who knows for certain passed away in 1927.

General agreement exists on which entrance Elijah likely used, one today called the "Carbide Entrance" which sits immediately to the west of the Main Entrance. Carbide is a substance that even today is often burnt in special lamps for exploring caves. Early cave guides stored their carbide inside the Carbide Entrance. The stream he followed out of the Cave exits at the main entrance where cave tours begin. One author speculated that Elijah entered at the Carbide, then went straight out the Main Entrance. That's also entirely possible, and likely prudent for Elijah, but would make for a total journey in the Cave of no more than about eighty feet, one without any total darkness. Not much of a story there. Elijah never stated how far he went into the Cave on that first trip, and likely couldn't remember, what with the adrenaline rush and all. Of course, if the details had been documented it would not allow for so much speculation. The gaps in the story lend more room for our imaginations.

So does it matter what the actual facts of the original event of Elijah's finding the cave are? Some details, yes, but either way it still stands as a great story, and since those facts cannot be completely ascertained, then the story takes precedence. And besides, who are we to discount Elijah? We weren't there. Neither was anybody else for that matter, except Bruno and the bear, and they're not talking.

Alright, Elijah Davidson found a cave. What's so important about that? Oregon Caves has become notable for a number of reasons. Because of its remoteness from other caves and the unusual environment there, the Cave contains as many or more endemic species of animals – those found *only* in the Cave – than any other cave in the United States, at least 7 endemics.

Found within the dark depths have also been one of the oldest Grizzly bear skeletons in North America, over 50,000 years old, and the most northerly Ice Age jaguar skeleton ever found, carbon-dated to 38,600 years old. Though the national monument and preserve is fairly small in size, about seven square miles, the rocks of the national monument, just like the forest above, are as complex and diverse as probably any place you will find in the National Park System. It's an amazing puzzle for a geologist. Some people, including cave guides, make a big deal out of it being a marble cave, and that is a bit special. But what's really special about the marble is that it preserves an important time in Earth's history, when there was a mass extinction at the end of the Permian period, over 200 million years ago.

On the human side, Oregon Caves also contains a prime example of "National Park Architecture" where buildings were constructed of native materials and built in a way to blend with the natural setting, in this case primarily the Oregon Caves Chateau (1934) and Chalet (1923). The list could go on, but this Cave that Elijah Davidson found so many years ago and the monument established around her, shine as a true gem in the necklace of the lovely, mysterious Siskiyou Mountains of southwestern Oregon.

Focus: Native People Of The Caves Region

Elijah Davidson was the first person we *know* to have entered the Oregon Caves. In the spring of 2009, a Caves Employee found an arrowhead in sediments that had come from the Cave. It does not prove that the Indians who made it entered the Cave, however, as it could have been washed in or come into the Cave inside of an animal that died there. However, it is very likely that well before Elijah Davidson ever knew of Oregon, native people of the area found and possibly made use of the Cave.

Evidence of Indians in Oregon dates to about 15,000 years ago, and the area of southwestern Oregon has likely been inhabited for a significant period of time. The primary groups of the region include the Takelma, Shasta, Tolowa, Galice/Applegate, Yurok and Karuk, with the Takelma likely associated with the immediate Oregon Caves area. They have a rich culture based on hunting, salmon fishing, and weaving beautiful baskets. They grew tobacco, and gathered many plants, including blue camas bulbs and acorns, their major forms of starch. The people lived mostly in the valleys along the rivers, not on the steep slopes of the Caves area, but visited the high country to gather plants and hunt. In the summer they lived in grass huts, but when winter rolled around they stayed in much warmer dugout houses covered with sugar pine planks. As previously stated, no conclusive evidence proves their knowledge of the Caves, but it was their backyard for a long time. Scarcity of evidence in such an environment, steep and lush, would be more expected than not.

*Yurok basket weaver Lena Hurd with an exhibit at Oregon Caves
(Photo courtesy of OCNM & P, Museum and Archives Collections)*

*Irma Thompson, Elijah's granddaughter
(Photo courtesy of the Thompson family)*

CHAPTER FIVE

Irma's Tale

Summer Davidson and his wife, Eva, gave birth to a girl by the name of Irma in 1910. In the summer of 2001 I traveled to Stockton, CA, to meet her and discuss her famous grandpa. When I arrived at the white house on a quiet residential street, I rang the bell. She came to the door quickly and looked up at me. I introduced myself. She responded with, "You portray my grandfather? He was just a little guy." I'm a bit over 6 feet tall. She offered tea or coffee, but since it was a warm summer day, I went for water. Her daughter Jeanne was with her, and after we chatted for a few minutes, she went about taking care of the place while Irma and I talked. She was a sweet woman and we had a lovely chat, mostly me listening to her stories and recollections. I recorded the chat, with her permission, of course, and later sent her a transcription of the conversation. Later she re-wrote the transcription, which gave it a better narrative flow. The following is her story of life with Grandpa. In her words you can catch more of the flavor of the people and the time in which they lived.

I first met Grandpa Elijah in the summer of 1915. I had turned five on January 29th of that year, and Grandpa was sixty-six. Grandma Minerva had died some time after they returned from Alaska, so Grandpa lived alone on a farm in Williams, Oregon. This may have been the farm and the house where some of their children were born.

We were living in Sacramento, California, when Grandpa wrote to my father saying that he needed help on the farm. My parents decided to go to Oregon. My mother, my brother Alpha, and I went first. My dad came later. He stayed to finish his job, to pack, and to bring our belongings.

We moved into the house where Grandpa was living. I was told it was Uncle Henry's house. Henry Boat was the husband of Olivia, Elijah's sister. It was a big old, gray house, with bedrooms upstairs, one bedroom downstairs, a parlor, and a large kitchen/dining room.

The farm was situated at the base of Grayback Mountain. A few hundred yards from the forest stood an age-weathered barn. It was separated from the house by a backyard where a big branching tree provided shade in the afternoon. When my daddy came, he made me a rope swing hanging from a limb of that tree.

Below the house and to the west, fields had been cleared for farming. Stumps of large trees dotted the edges like sentinels holding back the forest. Water was plentiful from the snows on the mountain, keeping the forest lush and green.

The old house, however, had no inside plumbing. We used an outhouse, a two-holer, old and gray like the house. I don't remember where we got water. There may have been a well, but a little ditch ran along the side of the field below the house. It was filled with fresh, clean water that may have been a spring coming from the mountain.

Pigs, chickens, and geese had free rein in the backyard. Hens tended their baby chicks, and baby goslings ran around our feet. Now and then a hawk circled overhead and mother hens called their babies to cover.

Grandpa Elijah was not a very tall man and his slender build hid the fact of his great strength. He had to be powerful to lug those huge, heavy steel traps to the mountains, set them, and then kill and skin the "varmints" he trapped, some of them much larger and heavier than he was. Even loading the skins and meat onto his horse took a lot of muscle. The state of Oregon honored him by issuing him a perpetual hunting license because of his ability as a trapper. Grandpa had light brown hair and a mustache tinged with red from his Scottish ancestry. I don't recall the color of his eyes, but I think they were bright blue like my father, who had all the same hair coloring. I never saw him laugh out loud, but when he was amused he chuckled in his throat.

Grandpa knew the essentials of farming, but his heart was always out there, somewhere, looking for adventure. He liked my brother Alpha (he called him Alphie) and taught him many things about the forest. Once I saw Grandpa with a flat straw hat on his head. A long net covered the hat and him down to his knees. He and Alphie were going to get some honey out of a hollow tree where bees had made a nest. Alpha told us later that some bees got under Grandpa's net, and Grandpa was swatting them frantically. Alpha said, "Grandpa, I think I'm going to have to laugh." Grandpa said, "Laugh dammit, laugh." He didn't chuckle then, but I think he did later when the bee stings stopped hurting.

Elijah with friends and relatives.
The front row includes Elijah's later dog, Nimrod, Elijah (with hat and mustache) and Summer Davidson (with the flat hat). Irma Thompson stands immediately behind Elijah.
(Photo courtesy of the Thompson family)

Alpha learned how to hold a skunk so it couldn't activate its defensive evil-smelling odor (you hold it up by the tail and away from your body – don't try this at home). He was showing Mr. Hartley, a neighbor, how to do it. However, when the skunk got its hind feet on Mr. Hartley's leg, it did its thing. Alpha and Mr. Hartley weren't friends after that. Probably Grandpa chuckled when he heard that story.

I was getting used to and thoroughly enjoying our new life, when one day one of the pigs began chomping on a little gosling. With half of its body and its head sticking out of the pig's mouth, the poor little bird was peeping and crying for help. I got a big stick and beat on the snout of that big beast with all my strength, but he went on chomping, crunch, grunt, crunch, grunt, ignoring my whacks. How I hated that pig! The little gosling went to goose heaven, but that pig's fate was yet to come.

Some evenings we sat around the big wood stove in the kitchen and Grandpa told stories of his hunting experiences. Alpha and I listened spellbound, eating apples or some of Grandpa's jerky, the best in the world. One story I didn't like was about some bear cubs he had found. He tied them to a tree and then spanked them until the mother bear came. Of course he shot her. There were many stories, but that one remained in my memory.

Another story was about a gold mine they had in Gold Hill, Oregon (about 10 miles from Williams, where Elijah lived). This was long before I knew him. He didn't do any mining after 1915. They were sluice mining, washing the ore in a controlled stream of water. Someone above them had the water rights and shut off their supply. That action forced them to close the mine. He also told about when they went to Alaska, going to Nome by dogsled. They had to put booties on the dog's feet to cross the ice.

We often had visitors. Two of Grandpa's friends became my very best friends. I suspect they came to sample my mother's cooking. One was Jess Sharp, who would come and play Parcheesi with me. He told us proudly that he had held the stirrup of Belle Starr when she came through town probably seeking a hideout. Belle was a notorious lady bandit. Another friend was Dick Rowley. He did marvelous woodcarvings. In later life he became a guide at the Caves (from 1913 to 1954). Just before his death he was in the Grants Pass hospital where he met his son, whom he had never known.

Grandpa was working in a field one day with a horse drawn springtooth harrow, a device like a rake with wide sharp claws that are supposed to dig into the soil to make furrows for planting. The claws weren't digging into the hard, dry ground. Grandpa said, "Irmie, come and sit on the prongs to weigh them down." I climbed on, but it didn't work. I wasn't heavy enough. Grandpa must have thought of another way, however, because we had a bumper crop of grain that year. I remember the men tossing the hay into the big wagon, and from there into the barn loft. When the last load went into the barn, it started to rain. My mother said it was an act of God.

Mom and Grandpa had some royal battles over politics. She was a Democrat. She told me that Grandpa once said, "I'd vote for a Republican if he was a little yellow dog!" I think he liked to tease her. She was a beautiful lady with a mind of her own. But they were really good friends. Grandpa listened to Mom when she said they should plant root vegetables when the moon was turning dark, and vegetables like corn and beans should be planted when the moon was getting brighter. It worked. We always had plenty of good vegetables. Mother was also a good Christian, and no doubt she persuaded Grandpa to think about where he was going to spend eternity.

Grandpa had many talents. He knew how to operate on animals to neuter them. One day I looked into the downstairs bedroom. It was filled with Rhode Island Red baby chicks. Grandpa and Mother were going to turn them into capons. The reason I think Grandpa was involved in this venture is because Mom didn't know how to neuter the chicks. When the capons grew up, they became large beautiful birds with long tail feathers, but no cockscombs; large plump bodies but they didn't lay eggs. However they made wonderful mothers for the baby chicks. Their size scared away the hawks. Mom and Grandpa thought they would make a killing selling the capons to the neighbors for their virtues and/or as fryers, but the neighbors weren't interested in hens that didn't lay eggs.

Dates and times don't register on a five year old, so I don't remember when Great Uncle John, Grandpa's brother, came to live with us. It was after my father came bringing chocolate and peppermint sticks. Uncle John was very sick and in a bed in our parlor. My mother said that she and my father were going to take care of him so that he wouldn't have to go to a hospital. That seemed to be a signal for Grandpa to go to the mountains to check his traps. He had a new Airedale dog. My mother named him "Nimrod," which she said meant "Mighty Hunter." Grandpa liked the name and Nimrod liked the part, so off they went.

Uncle John didn't take very long. When he died, Uncle Barty (Thomas Barton) came. He and my dad went into the woods searching for Grandpa. They found him and brought him home. It surprised me when Grandpa went in, looked at Uncle John, and with a trembling voice, kissed his brother and said, "Goodbye John." It was a new facet of Grandpa's nature I saw that day.

Lots of relatives arrived. I remember three great uncles, Uncle Jay, Uncle Grundy, and Uncle Carty. I especially remember Stella Davidson, Uncle Carty's daughter. She was in her late teens, sweet and charming, and very kind to a little girl, me. She slept with me on a bed at the end of the dining room. I have never forgotten her.

After Uncle John died, we moved to a house on the far side of the farm near Williams Creek. The house belonged to Joe and Maggie Boat, the son and daughter-in-law of Uncle Henry and Aunt Olivia. I don't remember ever seeing them, but a young brother, Chester Boat, visited us often.

Uncle Bartie, his wife Lillie, and their three children, Clive, Irene, and Ella, moved into Uncle Henry's house. Grandpa moved to his two room house up the road past the schoolhouse and the Vineyard ranch. There he had a small piece of land, a smokehouse, and a small orchard. We visited him often. When we moved to Joe Boat's house, Alpha and I started attending school in the one room schoolhouse. Alpha was in the seventh grade and I started first grade. Our teacher was Miss Ellistead, age nineteen. Some of the boys in the seventh and eighth grades were her age, and less interested in learning than in dating her, but she kept them in line. She was still there when we left.

One summer it came time to slaughter the pigs. I don't want to write about it except to say that Grandpa knew exactly what to do. The other men helped. I watched at a distance, horrified and fascinated, with bad dreams later. But I realize that these are things you have to do if you live on a farm.

I believe we lived in Oregon about four years. The summer of 1919, Mom decided she had enough of outdoor plumbing. She said, "Patsy," her name for my dad, "we've got to get out of here." My dad thought so too. He bought a used Ford, and we left for Stockton where my cousin Grace lived.

We went up to see Grandpa the summer of 1925. A girlfriend, Rowena Wright, and her family went with us. Grandpa was a bit perturbed at the gang that invaded his small space, but we had a beautiful night filled with shooting stars. We also visited the Oregon Caves. I had never seen them. Two young college boys were acting as guides. As interesting as the Caves were, I'm afraid the handsome guides distracted Rowena and me. They asked to show us the Caves that evening, but my mother said, "No!"

Grandpa came to Stockton the following year. One of our local papers interviewed him and gave him a nice write-up. I also believe he got to see Sarah Godwin, his sister. She lived about 30 miles away on a grape ranch near Concord, California.

A while after Grandpa went home he contracted cancer. My mother went up and she and Aunt Lillie (Barty's wife) took care of him until he died on September 9, 1927. Grandpa Elijah was buried in the Sparlin Cemetery (in Williams). The Sparlins were relatives of Grandma Minerva Farris.

Writing this and hearing what others have said about my grandfather Elijah, has given me a new perspective of him. I had always thought that he was sort of a hermit. He wasn't at all. Now I understand that losing his young son and the death of Minerva brought grief and change to his life. I wish I had known him earlier and longer. It's sad that so much separated us.

My four years in Williams Creek, Oregon, affected my whole life. I fell in love with the woods, the flowers popping up each spring, the evergreens, the firs, the cedars, and magnificent pines dominating the scene, and the creek where I played for hours making pools, trying to catch the minnows, and once in a while getting pinched by a crawdad.

No wonder Grandpa loved the forest. I understand now. He found so much beauty and peace there.

    Irma Thompson
    August 24, 2002

CONCLUSION

What more common archetype of the Wild West does America seem to value more than the rugged individual, alone in Nature, making his living off the land? Elijah embodied that ideal to a tee. He worked the soil as a farmer and was expert at reading the signs around him in the weather and the land, telling him when to plant and when to harvest. When he wasn't farming, he spent day after day in the mountains hunting and trapping to make a living for his family down in the valley, making use of the meat and selling the skins for bounty. And he was good at it, very good. He seemed to almost think like the animals at times. He knew how to cook that meat to perfection, from all accounts. He was a man of action, not words, though when he did speak up, people listened. He came from a family of people involved in education, so he had book learning, but he also had the education that only experience can truly teach. So yes, he embodied that archetype, yet he was not grandiose about it, preferring the simplicity of daily life and chores, doing what needed to be done.

Each of us wonders what kind of a legacy we will leave behind. Today, part of Elijah's legacy can be seen every time another family passes through the entrance of Oregon Caves National Monument, every time those entering the Cave feel the cool air in their faces at the Cave entrance and hear the stream rushing under their feet, every time people gaze in awe at the cave formations, and every time people delight to the story of that first known discovery of the place. While it's true that Elijah Davidson was not involved in the conservation of the Cave, its setting aside as a national monument, the fact that he did not publicize his discovery, and try to cash in on it, lent a slow progress to its discovery by the masses, which, in turn, kept the Cave from being more damaged than it was. Elijah was a man who disliked crowds of people, and had no inclination to turn the place into a circus the way many a cave has been. The remoteness of the Cave and the difficulty of arriving there from the nearest population centers also, of course, played a role in the lack of a rapid influx of visitors, but had Elijah been a different kind of man, I'm sure he could have profited handily at the Caves' expense.

Elijah Davidson's legacy can also be seen in the words of his granddaughter Irma, when she talks of how her time with him affected her whole life and gave her a deep appreciation for the beauty, the grandeur, and the peace of the natural world around her. For this ol' bounty hunter was also a family man, who helped raise six children, who touched their lives with his appreciation of the natural world, and blessed his grandchildren in the same way. Minerva and Elijah named three of those children after the seasons, one also including the name 'Forest.' Their lives had been tied to those seasons, that magnificent forest. He was also a feeling man who grieved the loss of one son taken too soon, and the loss of his dear wife, who weakened from the rigors of life in Alaska. He sought his solace, his healing, in the mountains and forests he loved.

Though we may not be Elijah's children, his relations, we, too, can be part of that legacy. Go to the Oregon Caves and breathe the damp cave air, let yourself really notice the texture of the flowstone, the marble, and walk the trails to find the peace and natural quiet of those magnificent forests Elijah so loved. Go without expectations, shut off your cell phone (they don't work well up there anyhow), and let the place become part of you.

*One of Elijah Davidson's hunting parties.
Elijah is on the far left.*

*(Photo courtesy of OCNM & P, Museum
and Archives Collections)*

APPENDIX I

History of the Discovery of the Marble Halls of Oregon

By E.J. Davidson, Provolt, Oregon

Originally published in the Quarterly of the Oregon Historical Society *in September 1922. Used by permission of the OHS.*

I had quite an experience that day and well remember something of the time. As to dates I cannot be quite sure, but I think it was the year 1873, in the month of October. A crowd of six, including myself, planned for a hunt in the Siskiyou Mountains. We packed several horses with provisions and our camping outfit, took our way up the middle fork of Williams Creek along a dim, brushy trail, then took our course through the open woods, crossing over the divide at the head of the creek, then down to Sucker Creek, where we halted for a short time and disposed of a much-needed lunch prepared for the occasion.

After lunch we continued on our way, which was anything but a smooth path. With a big mountain staring us in the face, and in many places almost perpendicular and no way around, we trudged on our weary way, trying to reach the top. Not a word was said, not a breath to spare, but all moved on in silence. Early in the evening we came to the Mountain Meadows, directly under the old noted Greyback Mountain. And say, I want to tell you, it was an ideal camping place. Our faces soon lost their tired, weary expression and lighted up with pleasure at the thought of tomorrow's hunt. All got busy and very soon we had a comfortable camp – everything in readiness for a good night's sleep.

Armed with our muzzle-loading rifles, we started early the next morning for our hunt. Every fellow was to select his own direction in which to follow. Something seemed to tell me to take the course that eventually led to the discovery of the caves. Picking up my rifle and taking my famous bear dog, Bruno, I started down the middle fork of Sucker Creek and then across to another creek. Knowing my dog so well, he gave me to understand there was something above. I at once, with the eagerness that only an old hunter can feel, slipped through the brush hoping to catch sight of something, and as I cautiously crept along I spied a large buck with his head well elevated in the air. I quickly leveled my gun, holding high his shoulder with a full bead, and let drive. At the crack of the gun the deer leaped into the air and was soon out of sight. Feeling sure I had hit him some, I told my dog to give chase. He was off like a flash and in less than a minute had the deer going down the mountain like double-geared lightning and into the canyon below. Being somewhat swift myself on a down-hill push, I was soon at the spot where a desperate struggle was taking place. Knowing the fight could not last long, as Bruno had his favorite hold on the animal's left leg, I waited for the end to come. Soon the buck fell and his heels went into the air. Bruno jumped for his throat quick as a flash; at the same time I seized a fore leg, threw it over his horns and with my hunting knife severed the jugular. It was then I discovered the wonderful head of horns. There were two perfect horns on one side and one on the other. The horns are still to be seen at Ad. Helm's place of business in Jacksonville.

Everything seemed to be leading me to the cave; for as I turned from my buck, I again found my dog with uplifted head and staring eyes directed into a clump of trees, waiting for the word "Go." I sprang for my gun and gave the word. He was off like lightning, while I followed as quickly as possible, and soon found myself in front of a large hole in the mountain. I could hear sounds of fighting coming from the far back in the mountain. Undecided as to what to do, I stood waiting, when my dog gave vent to a weird, agonizing howl as if he were in great pain. Hesitating no longer, I rushed into the opening and soon found myself coming up against sharp crags on the wall. I soon decided it was a hard chase to pursue without a light and, thinking of a few matches that I had in my old fashioned shot-pouch, very soon had a light and, to my surprise, found I was in some sort of cave; but losing no time in looking around, as the fight was being continued, I struck match after match, thinking I would soon be at the scene of the struggle. But no; my matches were gone! I turned to go back, but could see no rays of light. With the deafening howls and groans coming to my ears from somewhere near, made me think were I only out I would not attempt such a thing again. I finally found my way back to a running stream of water and, following it, came to the mouth of the cave. I waited anxiously for Bruno to come, and very soon he came splashing down the creek, and but for a few scratches was unhurt.

Neither I nor my dog were satisfied with the outcome of the fight, so I determined to take another chance; but as it was now well on in the evening, decided to go back to camp and return on the morrow. Before going I conceived the idea of placing the buck that I had just killed near the entrance of the cave, knowing Bruin would be sure to come out for food and, after eating all he could, would, as is their habit, lie down by the remaining part, which would give me a chance to kill him.

The next morning I returned very early to the scene of my encounter of the previous day and, just as I had anticipated, found the monstrous black bear lying near the carcass of the deer.

*(Photo courtesy of OCNM & P,
Museum and Archives Collections)*

APPENDIX II

A Timeline of Events for Oregon Caves and Elijah Davidson

1849 - Elijah Jones Davidson born on January 22 in northwestern Illinois.

1850 - Davidson family travels west on the Oregon Trail, settles in Portland, OR.

1852 - First white settlement in the Rogue Valley area.

1855 - The Davidson family relocates to Monmouth, OR.

- Rogue River Wars.

1866 - Elijah Barton Davidson moves his family, including Elijah Jones, to the Williams, OR area, settling at Missouri Flat.

1870 - July 4, Elijah Jones Davidson marries Minerva Farris.

1871 - Anna Geneva, Elijah and Minerva's first child, is born. They have 6 children in total.

1874 (?) - Elijah Jones discovers Oregon Caves while on a hunting trip.

1877 - Elijah returns to the Oregon Caves with William Fidler and others. Fidler writes the first published account of a trip to and through the Caves.

1884 - Professor Thomas Condon and his students tour the Caves.

1886 - Walter Burch, who had claimed the land around the Caves, opens a tiny passageway near the 110 entrance and discovers the bulk of the Cave.

1888 - Burch has left the Caves due to financial reasons.

1890 (?) - What would become the Oregon Caves Improvement Company started. They led two highly publicized expeditions in 1891 and 1894 and established the name "Oregon Caves." They did extensive damage to the Caves. The company dissolved in 1894.

1906 - Elijah, his wife, and daughter move to Nome, Alaska.

1907 - The Siskiyou Forest Reserve set aside as federal land on March 2. This included the Oregon Caves.

- C.B. Watson and Joaquin Miller visit Oregon Caves. Miller writes a major article about the Caves and Watson pushes to get the Caves protected.

1909 - July 12, President William Howard Taft establishes Oregon Caves National Monument

- Elijah and his family return from Alaska.

1910 - Irma Thompson, granddaughter of Elijah, born in California.

1913 - Dick Rowley hired on as guide to Oregon Caves.

- Elijah's wife, Minerva, passes away.

1922 - First road to the Caves completed. One tunnel on the tour route completed.

- Elijah publishes his account of his discovery of the Caves.

1923 - Chalet built at Oregon Caves to house guests.

1926 - Cabins built for more accommodation.

1927 - September 9, Elijah Jones Davidson succumbs to cancer at the age of 78 and is buried at the Sparlin Cemetery in Williams, OR.

1931 - Exit tunnel of the Caves completed.

1934 - Oregon Caves Chateau completed.

1954 - Dick Rowley retires.

2001 - The author comes to Oregon Caves when park rangers return to conducting cave tours for the first time in many years. Prior to that they were mostly led by a private company.

2014 - Oregon Caves National Monument additionally becomes a National Preserve when nearly 4000 acres of National Forest land is added to the Monument, protecting the watershed for the Caves.

The author in caving mode

ACKNOWLEDGMENTS

I offer special thanks to the friends and family of Elijah Davidson, especially the late Irma Thompson and her children Jeanne and Bruce, to Barbara Jean and George Koch, for memories, family info, and photos of the man himself. Thanks also to the late Babe Fields and his wife Barbara. Babe's recollections added another perspective on Elijah's status in the community. Also thanks to George Herring, Jason Walz, Sierra Heimel, and others at Oregon Caves National Monument and Preserve for access to their historical files, and for providing the maps needed for the book. Of course I must give thanks posthumously to Elijah Davidson, for without him there is no story. I also give thanks to Oregon Caves herself for the many years of beauty and wonder she has given to me. I also thank my editor and publisher, Ryan Forsythe, for pushing me to do better.

VISITING OREGON CAVES NATIONAL MONUMENT AND PRESERVE

Mailing Address: 19000 Caves Hwy
 Cave Junction , OR 97523

Phone: 541 592-2100

For the most updated information on cave tours and other items of interest, see the National Park Service website at **www.nps.gov/orca**.

Oregon Caves National Monument and Preserve is open year-round, though the cave itself is closed during the winter for bat hibernation. Generally tours of the Cave run from late March to late October and Discovery Tours (regular tours) last 90 minutes. Besides the regular tours, they also offer Candlelight and Off-Trail Tours during the busy summer months. Discovery Tours are considered moderately strenuous requiring the negotiation of over 500 stairs, some without railings, and bending as low as 45 inches in some passageways. Children must be taller than 42 inches to attend a Discovery Tour.

The visitor center within the national monument and preserve is only open when cave tours are in operation. To prevent the spread of White Nose Syndrome, a deadly disease for bats, please do not bring clothes (even washed clothes), shoes, or equipment used in any other cave, mine, or anything underground, when you come to Oregon Caves. Besides the cave tours, there are also wonderful hiking trails through the old growth forests of the national monument and preserve.

www.ingramcontent.com/pod-product-compliance
Lightning Source LLC
Chambersburg PA
CBHW061804070526
44586CB00023B/2700